the DEVIL'S THESAURUS

the DEVIL'S THESAURUS

Samuel Faulk

Andean Publishing
New York, NY

Copyright © 2023 by Samuel Faulk

All rights reserved. No part of this publication may be reproduced, distributed or transmitted in any form or by any means, including photocopying, recording, or other electronic or mechanical methods, without the prior written permission of the publisher, except in the case of brief quotations embodied in critical reviews and certain other noncommercial uses permitted by copyright law. For permission requests, write to the publisher, addressed "Attention: Permissions Coordinator," at the address below.

Andean Publishing
1420 York Avenue
New York, NY 10021
www.andeanpublishing.com

Publisher's Note: This is a work of fiction. Names, characters, places, and incidents are a product of the author's imagination. Locales and public names are sometimes used for atmospheric purposes. Any resemblance to actual people, living or dead, or to businesses, companies, events, institutions, or locales is completely coincidental.

Book Layout © 2023 Jeremy Taylor
www.instagram.com/jeremy.taylor.ny

Library of Congress Control Number: 2022915735
The Devil's Thesaurus/ Samuel Faulk.— 1st ed.
ISBN 978-1-7361277-9-7 | Paperback

As soon go kindle fire with snow,

as seek to quench the fire of love with words.

~William Shakespeare

the DEVIL'S THESAURUS

SAMUEL FAULK

Abandon, v.

The wheels of the car
spun out in the driveway.

Our biggest fight;
I never thought it would be
the last time I ever saw you.

As the rain began to fall, I remember
hoping this wouldn't be the end.
I prayed you'd come back to me.

***Restraint*, n.**

All the words I
should not
have said
blossomed
in my mind.

If only had I
used your crimson scarf
to cover my mouth
outside the bedroom.

Abnormal, adj.

It was like I didn't know
you anymore.

A stranger in my bed for
a long time now.

I'm just too scared
to look into your eyes
and ask
Who are you?

Customary, adj.

Every Christmas we stop by
my mom's house.
I guess I never asked;
it just became a habit.

We gather around the table,
eating smoked ham and pecan pie.
We act like our lives
are not in shambles.

We act like the silence and
my parents' divorce
isn't prophecy.

Acceptance, n.

You have a lazy eye.
It was the first thing I noticed
after your smile.

You were as self—
conscious as I am
about my height.

It took a few months
until you casually
kissed me and whispered,
You're not that short.

***Refusal*, n.**

It was far before my time,
a different city and a different man.
A party with too many drinks.
Your entire body screamed *No*.

Years later, you still tremble
as you lie down next to me,
even though I always ask permission.

Adopt, v.

Our first pet was a guinea pig,
named, sarcastically, Piggers.

You never knew, but when we got him
was the night I stopped sleeping.

Even after he died,
his squeaking voice kept me awake.

Like my memories do now.
I haven't slept in years.

Neglect, v.

The morning after you left,
I noticed the flowers
on the windowsill
were dead.

Of all the things we ignored,
new haircuts, sundresses,
muttered words, each other...

Of all the things I never noticed,
why did the flowers have to die?
Where can I find beauty now?

Allure, v. and n.

It was the way you spoke
of your passions.
Your eyes would light up.

Hughes,[1] Whitman,[2] Plath.[3]
The poets who described a world
you wished to live in.

I always wished that
I could be as
passionate about anything
the way I was about you.

---

1 Let America Be America Again
2 Fast Anchor'd Eternal O Love!
3 *Mad Girl's Love Song*

Repulse, v. and n.

I haven't always hated
tongue rings, but now
I despise them.

Perhaps it's the idea
you needed to draw attention
to something more than your speech.

Or that my lips were not enough.
Or maybe it's a message
telling the world how dangerous
a "silver-tongue" can be.

Banish, v.

It wasn't the first time
you kicked me out,
but this time it was
winter.

I wandered the streets,
hoping that you would call
before the weather
crept into your soul.

Maybe it already has?

Allow, v.

They warned me to guard it,
keep it locked up, safe, out of reach.

After all it could easily be
stolen, broken, or burned.

But when I met you,
you didn't have to ask.

I freely gave away my heart
without a second thought.

Barter, v. and n.

I had never prayed—or begged—
as hard as I did That Night.

When God did not answer,
I tore the room apart.

I threw everything to the curb
and hung a sign:
For Sale: BABY CRIB, NEVER USED.

Possess, v.

My name was on the lease.
I made more money.
I paid for college.

But I knew better
than to claim anything.
Your spirit will always be free.

Bereft, v. and adj.

I cannot imagine a world
without you in it.

Even now,
the truth of your absence
does not agree with my reality.

Happy, adj.

I did not know
a single word could hold
so many different meanings
until I met you.

Bitter, adj.

Coffee needs cream.
Dark chocolate needs sugar.

My life needs you.

Sweet, adj.

I'd never met someone who
enjoyed pistachio gelato
as much as I do.

Until you came along.

Brazen, adj.

The confidence with which
you cook surprised me.
You needed no help at all
for our first Thanksgiving together.

The turkey was perfectly moist,
but the stuffing was dry.
The mashed potatoes were like soup.
I ate every bite.

***Humble, adj.*

It took me years to admit
I hate tomatoes.

But you get them on pizza all the time!
you exclaimed, confused.

No, I replied, *I take them off.*
I was waiting for you to notice.

C

Candid, adj. and n.

Are the words we say
ever really honest?
When even the pictures
we have are posed?

Is there any honesty left
between the sheets,
or in the dark?

Guarded, adj.

You slept curled up
in the fetal position.
Arms hugged your chest.
Sometimes yours, sometimes mine.
I fit my body to the curve of yours
so we could both protect
your heart even
while asleep.

Caress, v.

Every bump,
bruise,
or scar
tells
a
story that
I want to read.
I trace my finger
along your
spine,
hoping to
unlock what
makes you so kind.

Scratch, v and n.

There's a mark on your left shoulder
between two freckles.
You won't tell me where it's from.

I wonder what else you hide
underneath your skin.

Carnal, adj.

The memories of all our
nights together—
and the thirst for your body,
the pull of your lips,
the curve of your hips—
stay locked in my mind,
playing on repeat.

Spiritual, adj.

I prayed at your altar.
I drank your wine.

I recited your creed
of what it meant to love.

I worshiped you
in the purest way I knew.

Celibate, n.

Me genoito![4]

---
4 First sentence of Romans 3:6 (KJV) in Greek.

Promiscuous, adj.

You started working late.
I thought nothing of it
until you began
wearing makeup.

Cheat, v. and adj.

How can I touch you,
knowing where you have been?

Your body has
lain in another's bed.
Your words have
soothed another's ear.

I know where your body has been.
What of your soul?
How far did you truly wander?

Honest, adj.

I've never admitted how loved
you made me feel the first time
you held my hand.

No one has ever held it before.
People assume it's broken.
How can I explain
the term "spastic palsy"
without fear of rejection?

Daze, v. and adj.

Every moment spent with you
is fuzzy and unfocused
as if by trying to remember,
I damaged the camera lens.

But the words you say
need no camera,
and the mic remains unbroken.

Expectant, n.

I often wonder if things
would have been different
if I chased you instead.

I knew you wanted me,
so I stopped running.

Deprive, v.

All the air is gone
as I struggle to breathe.
Why is it so cliché to think
that I could be
nothing without you?

Renew, v.

The springtime of the soul
comes when we need it most.
It gives me the strength
to carry on, even if only for today.

Desire, v. and adj.

All we ever want
is someone to laugh with
and hold at night.

The irony is
we do not know
what to do
once we find
the one who offers us
so much more.

***Antipathy*, n.**

We hate the one
we once knew and loved
but no longer recognize.

The worst is when
it is us who stares back
through a mirror
unbroken.

Doctrine, n.

I prayed at your altar.
I drank your wine.

I recited your creed
of what it meant to love.

Why then did nothing
wash away my sins?

Skeptic, n.

I should have seen the signs.
How could I have known
that you would meet *him*
at a party, with me there?

Part of me knew
when I started waking up
without you next to me.

Durable, adj.

Am I still a knight
when I have fallen?

My armor no longer shines.
It is beaten, tarnished,
scratched, and dulled.

But for my queen,
I stand once again
and fight in the shade
of poison arrows
as they fall.

Fragile, adj.

We danced around the words
for weeks before
they were spoken.

I can't remember
who said them first,
that declaration that
changed everything:
I love you.

𝓔

Eccentric, adj.

You had an ankle tattoo,
written in Elvish.

My music collection ranges from
Classic Rock to Swedish Pop.

Your hair never stayed the same
color for more than a month.

I offer my opinion to any stranger's
private conversation—unwanted or not.

How wonderful it was that we'd
found each other in a world full of crazy.

Normal, adj.

Sundresses and nature hikes,
Netflix and Domino's,
sharing books under the willow tree,
people-watching in the park.

It is the mundane
that we take for granted
once the dust settles.

Ensnare, v.

They say one "falls"
in love,
as if love is a trap set
in the woods, covered
by brittle leaves.

As if love is a pool of water
you can drown in.
As if I did not take
one look and jump.

You do not fall in love.
You take a running leap
and pray someone
will catch
you.

Release, v.

They talk about moving on
as if I can willingly stop thinking
about everything you were.

As if you will voluntarily
climb out of my head
and lock the
door behind
you.

Equality, n.

True fairness means
that the woman is not
the only one with scars.

True fairness means
I am broken, just like you.

***Opposition,* n.**

As the years slipped away,
so did you.

Even as we lay in bed,
you strained against me.

Clasping my body while
pushing me away with your eyes.

Love became a fever with no cure.

Erosion, n.

The parchment on which
my words of love are scrawled
crumbled before the ink dried.

The stone foundation
on which we stood
fell
        apart
long before either of us noticed.

Does rust have any purpose
besides reminding us of the damage
that comes from rain?

Fortify, n.

The Three Little Pigs do not need
to build a stronger house
until they see the threat
of the Big Bad Wolf.

When we feel safe, we act carelessly.

There is no fault in feeling safe
until a wolf is
at your door.

Eulogy, n.

How do words like "goodbye"
do you justice?
If we use it
when separated for hours?

How do I now say
"goodbye" for a lifetime
when I can't say "see you soon"?

Slander, n.

For all our faults,
I hope you speak well
of me in the end.

In my stories you are always
the angel I first saw.
Everyone deserves redemption.
Even when it is never sought.

Fable, n.

Icarus taught us to not fly
too close to the sun.

The Ugly Duckling taught us that
beauty needs to be nurtured.

Avoid Midas' touch lest you
become greedy for more than me.

If only our happy ever after
did not have to end.

Reality, n.

I cannot comprehend
the scent of your perfume

lingering on my pillow
after you have gone.

Love has driven us
all to madness.

Fervor, n.

We wrote our story in the fire
and gentle whispers of love.
Our tongues the quills,
our bodies the canvas.

Apathy, n.

There was never a moment when ardor for you did not burn within my chest.

I simply ran out of new ways to say "I love you".

Finesse, n.

I learned the subtle
cues of your body.
The curves of your hips,
the twinkle in your eyes.

The lines of your palms
spoke of destiny foretold.
You moved with such delicacy,
I feared you would break.

Ignorance, n.

Bliss only remains
until knowledge is acquired.

Like Eve in the garden of Eden,
I tasted the forbidden fruit
and marveled at its bitter taste.

We are naked in a world
where we are not as smart
as we once were.

Flourish, v.

The way you danced
in your summer dress
took my breath away.

You spun pirouettes,
sweeping arms
and poised legs.

You dare not open your eyes,
lest you fully know
your own beauty.

Don't worry—I never blinked.

Languish, v.

It was weeks after That Night
until I finally crawled out of bed.
Even then, my body
had more strength than
my heart ever did.

Fracture, n. and v.

Out of
broken
 ness—
comes beauty.

Whether your
body　　heals
stronger, or your soul
never heals
 at all.

Closure, n.

Will this chapter of our lives
ever truly be over?
With so much left unsaid?
How can I walk away,
when the ink has yet to dry?

Gallant, adj. and v.

You were surprised when
I arrived in a pinstripe suit,
a bouquet in hand, expecting
nothing from you.

I would simply smile because
even in sweatpants with frizzy hair,
you were my queen.

Cowardly, adv.

I was terrified
of not loving you enough.
I never had the time
to think of the reverse
until it happened.

Genuine, adj.

The ring on your finger,
with real diamonds,
was my grandmother's.

Is a gift the most authentic
thing about you?

Dishonest, adj.

Is it worse
to live in the web of lies
woven for our own protection
or face the harshest truth?

Glorious, adj.

We lay in a field
watching the sunrise.
As the lights spread
across the sky.

Stars disappeared
one by one,
only to return
in your eyes.

Meretricious,[5] *adj.*

There are certain words
that when found
surprise and intrigue you
by their definition.

How I wish this did not
fit you perfectly.

---

5 My surprise at this definition rivals only my fear that you would stand on a street corner and fulfill it.

Guilt, n.

If only trashy
television shows
were your only secret.

***Innocence*, n.**

There was a small black dot
on your white dress.

Slowly the stain grew
and you pretended not to notice.

Gluttony, n.

There is no regret from consuming too much of you. Only the pangs of hunger when you are gone.

***Satisfaction*, n.**

When you said,
*I have more books
than bookshelves*
I knew you were the one.

Habitual, adj.

Our lives became routines
of eating, working, and sleeping.
Soon we had no time for the things
that truly mattered,
like each other.

Spontaneous, adj.

I hate the cold,
but I will always
jump in snow piles,
barefoot,
with you.

Harangue, n.

I screamed at
the top of my lungs.
*How could you forget
the vows we made?*

I quoted, reasoned,
ranted and pleaded.
But your thoughts
were still on *him*.

Rave, v.

At the beginning,
We were ecstatic.
Together we told the world.

Heartfelt, adj.

The words[6] we whispered
to each other
in the dead of night
were the only truth
we ever needed.

---

6 See *Fervor pg. 64*

False, adj.

The day you accused me of cheating
was the day I discovered
that you secretly smoked cigarettes.

You locked us in the room and lit one
while screaming threats.
Asthma stopped my breathing,
smoke[7] covered my eyes.

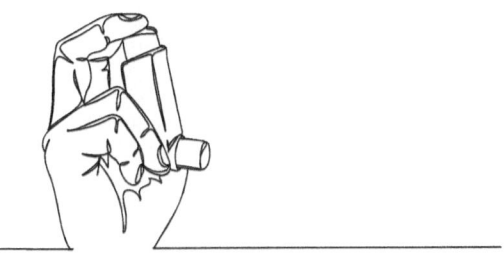

---
7 *Romeo and Juliet* (1.1 167-169)

Heathen, adj.

The Prodigal[8] was only
praised once he returned.
What would happen
if he never did?

Lord, help my unbelief.

---

8 Luke 15: 25-32

Sacred, adj.

We built an altar
to each other
of whispered dreams.

We piled it high with
thorns of insults
and burnt offerings of regret.

We chanted hymns of hope
in each other.

Heinous, adj.

One thing you
hated me for
was for never giving up.

As if I needed to break
so that you could be justified.

Magnificent, adj.

Our first kiss was like a dream.
Standing on the soccer field,
I held you close
until the sprinkler passed over.

In a seasonal drought,
it was the best I could do
to kiss you in the rain.

Idealism, n.

Our love was like
writing a novel
on a typewriter.

So many grand ideas ~~and risks~~,
with messy, scarred corrections.
And the original ~~still hidden~~ underneath.

We spent so long trying
to fix everything,
we don't even notice
we ran out of ink.

Pragmatic, adj.

We were both dreamers,
trying to find our way
in a world which
shot us down
from the
sky.

The harshest reality
comes from those who
were forced awake.

I no longer dream.

Ignoble, adj.

You started lying
about fancy dinners,
and drinks with friends.

I should have asked
why we stopped
going to our favorite bars.

Could I have handled the answer?
Would I have seen *him?*

Dignified*, *adj.

We didn't need
ball gowns and Armani suits
to show the world that
we were royalty.
All we needed was a dream.

Illuminate, v.

Light shone not from
your smile or your eyes,
but from your fingertips.

You brightened everything
you touched and pushed
away the darkness
for a little longer.

Obscure, adj.

It's in the healed scars,
the lines etched into our skin,
the calluses on our feet,
and the music in our head
that stories are told.

Immanent, adj.

It was my love of words
that caused me to start
this poem inside my head.
I never stop writing.

I will try
to put into words
exactly how I feel about you.

Extrinsic, adj.

Because we were young,
the world told us we wouldn't last.
Your family disliked me on the spot.
My friends were suspicious.

I often wonder what
we could've been if
we only listened to each other
and shut the world out.

Indulge, v.

I want to swim in your veins,
drink from your pool,
blend every part of me with you
until our souls touch.

Let me find the colors
of the rainbow
inside your eyes.

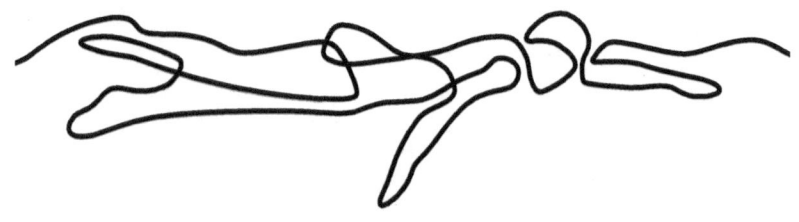

***Stifle*, v.**

I loved you even as
the poisonous words fought
to escape my mouth.

I held my breath.
Your feelings
were more important
than being right.

Jeer, v.

You asked me
what I thought of
your new dress and
this time I was honest.

Commend, v.

You were so relieved
when I stood up to your father
and told him to stop drinking.

Jejune, adj.

They laughed at us
for watching Disney movies.
We questioned where else
they learned about love.

Elegance, n.

As I watched you walk
down the aisle,
I finally knew what it meant
for a knight to lay down his life
for his queen.

Jilted, v.

In that one moment[9]
you threw me away,
when you called out
his name instead of mine.

---
9 Or was it even sooner?

***Cherished,* v.**

I knew I was special to you
when we shared a glance.
Then I realized it was
the same look
you give to a puppy
without a home.

Jubilant, adj.

I never knew that
craving Oreos and salsa[10]
could mean so much
or cause so much joy.

---

10 See *Rave* pg.89

Morose, adj.

Dark storm clouds formed
when I realized you were gone.

I never wished for this.
I never wished for rain.

Judicious, adj.

I ignored all the red flags
when we first met.
The rumors can't be true.

Even though I knew
something was wrong.
You've changed.

Every sweet word you said
drowned the voice in my head.
There's no one else.

I should have listened.

Temerarious, adj.

When I asked you
to move in with me
I had no plan.

Were you just as foolish
as me to say yes so quickly?

K

Keen, adj.

I learned everything
I could about you.

You cringe every time a car door slams,
because of your father.

The scar behind your left ear
came from protecting your sister.

A psychic once told you
that you would marry a Virgo.

If I remember all these things about you,
why don't you remember I'm a Leo?

Obtuse, adj.

Slowly it all blurred together,
like one too many glasses of wine.

This is why I started drinking,
so that you would notice me.

This is why I stopped drinking,
so there was something to notice.

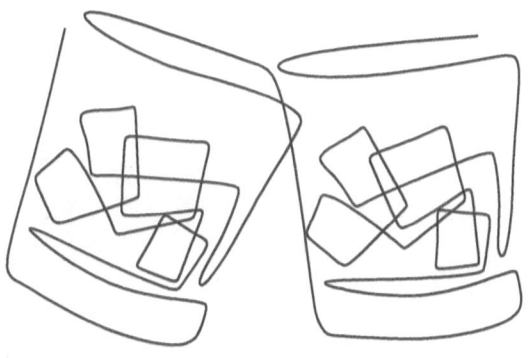

Kerfuffle, n.

I wanted you to scream;
I wanted you to fight for us.

You did nothing,
resigned to your fate.

I walked out the door,
hoping you would follow.

Tranquility, n.

You calmed the raging seas
within my mind
with your whispered words.

In your arms my neuroses fell away.
My fears and pain ceased.
I could exist without thought
even if just for a moment.

Kithe, v.

What more do I have to do
to prove my love?

Must I write in the sky,
or scream from the mountaintops?

When did my words become
not enough for you?

***Repudiate,* adj.**

I couldn't believe it when you told me.
The secret I had suspected for weeks.
I still can't accept this truth.
Him? How could this be?

Knavish, adj.

When you accused
me of cheating[11]
you "caught me" talking to your sister.

Merry Christmas,
I'm flying you home.

I never understood the phrase
"benefit of the doubt"
until I did not receive it.

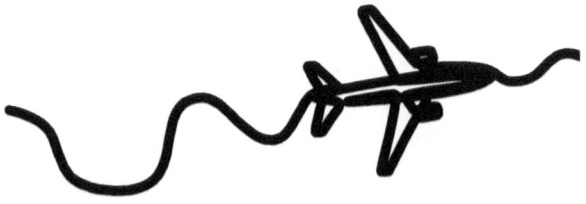

---
11 See *False* pg.91

Virtuous, adj.

Many forget that Eve
was not alone.
Adam watched as she sinned,
and fell from grace with his bride.

Knowingly, adv.

How do we go on
once we truly realize
the pain we caused
to the ones we love?

Inept, adj.

Perhaps we are all
stumbling through this life
until we find someone to lean on.

Laborious, adj.

Those who do not
work at love
do not truly
understand its cost.

Reticent, adj.

I knew about *him* for weeks
but I didn't say anything.

Not yet.
You deserved a chance
to explain yourself, at least.

Instead, I let the silence grow.
When did *nothing* become
our soundtrack?

Lacerate, v.

No one mentions how deep one's tongue can truly cut[12] when love turns to hate.

---

12 *Macbeth* (4.3.228-9)

***Mend**, v.*

Our fingers held threads of hope.
Stitching our lives back together.

Forcing the bones of our love
back into their rightful place.

Would the surgery succeed,
or had the infection spread?

Latent, adj.

It hides under our skin,
in the back of the mind.
Swims behind our eyes.

That one word we're afraid to utter
to another living soul.
Doubt.

Functioning, v.

We worked well together for so long,
like a well-oiled machine
of bills, chores, and healthy meals.

But is sustaining
our livelihood
truly living?

Livid, adj.

When I think about *him*
all I see is red.

Sanguine, adj.

The best night of my life wasn't
our honeymoon,
but just a regular Tuesday.

Where we sat next to each other
with a bottle of wine,
and talked about the future.

Lover, n.

How can mere words describe everything you meant to me?

Carper, n.

The way you sighed
each time I
left a smudge
on a clean dish
was worse than
if you screamed.

Mad, adj.

Aren't we all
a little crazy,
when we are
falling in love?

Sane, *adj.*

You laughed when I said,
*Pineapple does not
belong on pizza!*

I'm not even sure
why I was so adamant.

Magical, adj.

Light shone not from
your smile or your eyes,
but from your fingertips.

Stars disappeared
one by one,
only to return
in your eyes.

Ordinary, adj.

I stared out at the mountains
admiring the view.

To me they were beautiful,
to you they were a backdrop
filtered out of sight.

Mature, adj.

Over time, I stopped
jumping in snow piles
and eating gelato in February.

I thought I needed
to put such things behind me.
I wish I never stopped.

Raw, adj.

Will this pain
ever end?

Merry, adj.

Is it only at Christmas time
that we all feel warm and fuzzy?

What would it take
to feel this way forever?

Despondent, adj.

How can mere words describe
everything you meant to me?
Can words convey this ache in my soul?

Move, v.

You trained for months
to run a marathon.
You'd leave for hours
on Saturdays
to go running.

Or at least
that's what
you told me.

Stay, *v.*

That first night in our new house,
we slept on the floor, waiting
for the bed to be delivered.

We toasted with wine in paper cups,
thrilled to be in our forever home.

Narrow, adj.

Is the
road to
happiness as
thinly traveled
as the
road to
heaven? Is
it any
different?

***Spacious*, adj.**

We used   to   laugh
about how it   felt to   sleep
on a   king—sized mattress.

Lying on either side,   our hands
reaching across the chasm   of foam,
linen, pillows,   and springs.

The bed is
empty now.
As if cut
in half.
I   am   adrift
in an ocean
of foam, linen,
pillows and springs.

Natural, adj.

Holding you at night
was the simplest act,
as automatic as breathing.

Why can't I breathe anymore?

Simulated, *adj.*

You used to joke about *The Matrix*.
You'd say it was a glitch every time
I entered a room and forgot why.

Call me to pull you out of the Matrix!
I'm calling. Why won't you answer?

Neat, adj.

It was months after you were gone
before I invited friends into ~~our~~ my home.
They marveled at how clean the house was.
Surprised at my upkeep.

What they didn't see was the weeks before,
where grief overwhelmed basic needs.
Rock bottom is cold and filthy.

Untidy, adj.

Saturdays were my favorite day.
Even in sweatpants with frizzy hair,
you were my queen.

Chores piled up, but that didn't matter
because the coffee was hot
and the eggs were fresh.
All that mattered was we were together.

Night, n.

I started sleeping with
the door closed.
If I don't, sometimes
I wake up from
bumps in the night,
and for a single solitary moment
convince myself it's you
standing in the open doorway.

Day, n.

Sunlight peeked in through curtains
to signal a new morning.
I rolled over, reaching for a kiss.

You squealed, cursing my breath
and rolled out of bed.

Noisy, adj

You always played
pop music while cleaning,
loudly, to be heard above the A/C.

To be heard above me.
I'm sorry I never danced with you.
It was so loud I couldn't think.

Silent, adj.

Words of love spoken long ago
Never to be spoken again.

The silence I craved for so many years is deafening now.

Obedient, adj.

I checked all your boxes.
I wore the right clothes.
Said the right things.

I became who you wanted.
Why, then, did you no longer
want the man I became?

Recalcitrant, adj.

I stood in the doorway,
loose tie in my hand.

It's my first office party.
Please come with me.

You declined and made an excuse.
Little did I know it was *his* birthday.

Optimistic, adj.

Sometimes, when I roll over
in the middle of the night,
of course, I want you.[13]

But sometimes, I just want
to pull you closer to me.
To feel your warmth against my skin.

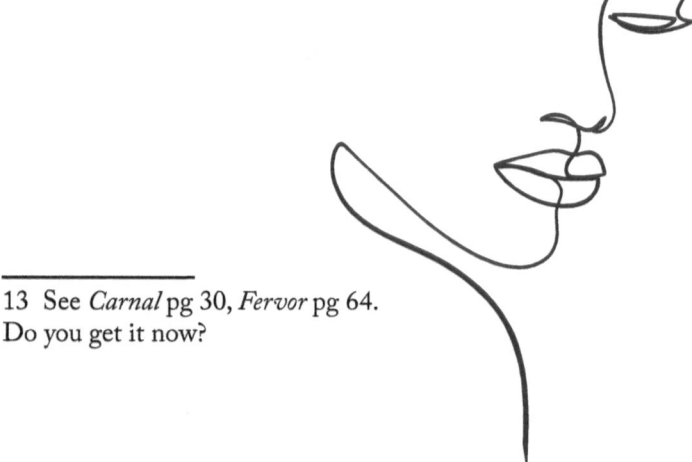

---
13 See *Carnal* pg 30, *Fervor* pg 64.
Do you get it now?

Disappointed, adj.

It was morning. You wore nothing
except my favorite T-shirt.
You frowned at the scrambled eggs,
because we were all out of milk.

They won't be fluffy.
They won't be the best, you said,
holding the spatula like a wand,
hoping for magic.

Obvious, adj.

Your screen name mentioned
your eyes, and that's what drew me.
Forest green reminds me of home.

Ambiguous, adj.

My screen name mentioned
being reborn, and my fire within.
Was it my abstraction that drew you
or the idea of hope?

Offer, v.

It was our third date
and I brought flowers.

I knew that roses
could be too much, too soon.
So I handed you a few white lilies
and hoped for the best.

Revoke, v.

Losing you is like having
a phantom limb,
aching at the point
of separation.

~~What happens when I go numb?~~

Omission, n.

I stopped making
your coffee in the morning.
After all, if my big sacrifices
were no longer noticed
how could the little ones be?

Include, v.

I was always excited when
you invited me out
with your friends.

We all had fun until
I noticed the whispering
behind my back.

Permanent, adj.

Silver rings forged in fire,
eternal   symbols of our
once in a lifetime love.

Vows made before God,
proof that this will
last forever.

Temporary, adj.

I never thought emptiness
would feel as heavy
as the absence of you.

I never thought emptiness
would feel as heavy
as the ring you left behind.

Persevere, v.

I can only say
I stayed for you
so many times
before it's a lie.

The truth is:
I stayed because
I had nothing ~~left to try.~~

Falter, v.

I stumbled back,
drink sloshing in my hand.

You did *what*
with *who?*

Poetry, n.

I found a poem you wrote
buried in a drawer, gathering dust.

It was about how much
you loved me. I wish I had known.
I wish I had seen this years ago.

Prose, n.

I still remember your sparkling smile and tinkling laugh from the night we met.
After coffee we took a walk.
Strolling along the river's edge we talked for hours, never wanting the night to end.
The river moved as slowly as our words, flowing endlessly.

Prevaricate, v.

The worst part about it all
is not that you lied to me.

It is simply that I believed you
too many times, for far too long.

Factual, adj.

I stared at the headlines
the day after That Night.
The irony was not lost on me.
President adds a new addition
To the White House Family!

Prudent, adj.

I was the first one to
walk around the house unclothed.
I always assumed you were shy.
Or did you have something to hide
even back then?

Reckless, adj.

For our sixth month together
I took us skydiving.

Was it trust or carelessness
that caused you to jump?

Quality, n.

The ring on your finger,
with real diamonds,
was my grandmother's.

Worth more than our
entire wedding.

How did it feel to have
that much responsibility?

Inferiority, n.

Nothing destroys a man quite like earning his love, then one day looking him in the eye and whispering, *You aren't worthy of me.*

Quell, v.

Slow dancing with you turned down the noise in my head. Constantly assessing balance and speed. In your arms my neuroses fell away. My fears and pain ceased. I finally felt safe, like I could never
fall.

Amplify, v.

The aftermath of an argument tends
to change even the little things.

Contented silence becomes
a frosty shoulder.
A closed door becomes
a slammed one.

Chores become angrily
washing dishes with the
crashing of plates and cups.

Is it really this loud
or is it all in our head?

Question, n.

How many times
can I ask *Why?*
before it becomes
a mantra?

Answer, n.

I never asked about *him*
because I feared
what you would say.

Quick, adj.

It all happened so fast.
The heat of my bed
is cooling now.
Fire became ash.

Sluggish,* *adj.

Even the jolt of fresh coffee is blurred and dull without you dancing in my kitchen.

Days fade into years.

Quiet, adj. and n.

When did *nothing* become
my soundtrack?
The silence I craved
for so many years
is deafening now.

Loud, adj.

I screamed[14] at the ceiling
until my voice gave out.

How could this happen?
Why aren't you here?
~~What do I do without you?~~

---
14 *Othello* (4.2.32-33)

Rare, adj.

We'd been dating for a while now
and this time you paid for my meal.
I'm sorry I was so surprised.
I'm not used to being
treated like an equal.

***Quotidian**, adj.*

Some days I enjoyed traffic.
It gave me time to think
and a few more minutes of time
to myself.

Recant, adj.

How can you say
you never loved me?
When I built my world
on the antithesis?

***Profess*, v.**

Instead of shouting from
the rooftops, I will scrawl
my thoughts on this paper.
I love you. I love you. I love you.

Romantic, adj.

The setting sun glinted, reflecting off the water. We stood on the cliff side watching baby seals play down at the water's edge. I looked you in the eyes and kneeled.

Practical, adj.

We replaced my junker car
after the wedding.
Time to settle down,
and be responsible.

What do I do with it now?
With so much ~~empty~~ space?

Rigid, adj.

The first time my father
visited our new home
he smiled, tapped the wall
with his shoe and said,

It's got good bones, it'll last.

Flexible, adj.

How far can we bend our
willful ignorance
before it breaks?

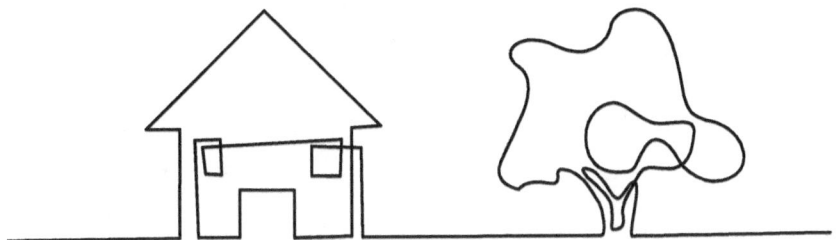

Rude, adj.

You're absolutely right.
She was way out of line.

***Courteous,* adj.**

I could always tell when
you had a bad day.

It took a few moments to drop
your customer service voice.

Scatterbrained, adj.

Sometimes I wake up
and reality hasn't hit me yet.
In that silver moment
between dreaming and daylight.

Then I reach over[15] to shake you awake
and my hand touches nothing
but the empty space
where you used to be.

---

15 See *Night* pg. 166

Shrewd, *adj.*

I sat there, spinning through all the
possibilities in my mind.

Calculating all the ways
this could go wrong.

In the end, though, you won me over.
We painted the room blue.[16]

---

16 See *Rave* pg. 89

Serious, adj.

You asked me to sit down
with a serious look on your face.
I have something to tell you.

My heart skipped a beat.
Is this it? Is this when you admit
what I already know?

You cracked a smile, chuckling at the joke.
I'm pregnant! You beamed.
Joy crashed with fear.

Trivial, adj.

I'm not even sure
why I was so adamant.

Maybe I just needed
to feel heard above the noise.

No, we're not telling my parents this early.

Strenuous, adj.

I told you
I don't like yoga.

Feeble, adj.

You thought my silence was acceptance.
The truth is, I didn't have
the strength to speak.

Let alone stop you
from walking out the door.

Supportive, adj.

I gleamed with pride
when you declared
you wanted to go to college.

It didn't matter what you studied,
as long as you found meaning.
I'm glad you chose Literature like me.

Abjure, v.

And I never drank again.
Not after what you did.

Synonym, n.

Isn't it wonderful
that we have so many
different words that mean
the same thing?
No wonder we get confused.

Antonym, n.

Apathy is the opposite of love.
Not hate, like many believe.
The act of slowly growing numb,
losing interest in the minutiae,
simply no longer feeling.

Taboo, n.

It turns out I wore
the wrong jersey
to the Super Bowl party.

***Encourage**, v.*

I was always so proud when you
asked me for help with your homework.

I knew you were embarrassed,
starting school so late.

But I knew you'd get better grades
than I ever did.

Telic, adj.

This time it was you who left.
After roaring insults and slammed doors
I've been wanting to leave for years.

***Indefinite,** adj.*

I never really knew what we meant by "See you soon." It seems so loose, languid.
Soon could mean minutes, days, years.
~~Or even longer.~~
I'll see you soon.

Thirst, n.

Avoid Midas' touch lest you
become greedy for more than me.
That silver tongue of yours begging
for another drop.
Desire is a beast never satisfied.

Fertile, adj.

When you told me the news,
I was shocked and confused.
I started counting the days.

Timorous, adj.

On our first date, in real life,
we met for coffee.

Stumbling over small talk,
sipping cappuccinos.

Would I have been so nervous
if I knew what was to come?

***Forthcoming*, adj.**

I have something to tell you.
My heart skipped a beat.
Is this it? Is this when you admit
what I already know?

~~I'm not ready.~~

Tolerance, n.

Every time I noticed you
didn't start the full dishwasher,
I never said a word.
I just pressed the button
and sighed my own sigh.[17]

---

17 See *Carper* pg. 143

Contempt, n.

When I first found out about *him*,
I tried very hard to hate you.
Instead, all I could feel
was sadness at losing
someone who helped
me find myself.

U

Unconscious, n.

It turns out we both
talk in our sleep.

I mutter about books and stories.
You whisper about . . . me.

Aware, adj.

What I wouldn't give
to go back to a time
before I knew about *him*.

Back to a time before
I knew the bitter taste
of the fruit.[19]

---

19 See *Ignorance* pg. 67

Unique, adj.

Car rides, hikes, and sunsets.
In the fleeting moments where

time falls through the hourglass
one grain of sand at a time,

it is here where we learn
who we truly are
and what
makes us
family.

Commonplace, adj.

It's all the little things:
asking me to cook bacon
because I "do it best".

The way you hold my hand
while you're driving,

or pull my glasses off my face
just to stare deeper into my eyes.

It's all the little things
that create love.

Unknown, adj.

Did you ever truly
love me the way
I loved you?
Or was I alone
like I am now?

Proverbial, adj.

"There is no difference between a wise man and a fool when they fall in love."[18]

---

[18] English Proverb

Upset, v.

It was our first fight
after moving in together.

You kept repeating,
In my family, we did it this way!

I chuckled. *It's the law.
You have to do it this way!*

Stabilize, v.

I held you while you cried.
It's okay. We'll get another pet.
He won't be forgotten.
Not in this family.
Not our Piggers.

Urge, n.

Sometimes when I roll over
in the middle of the night
I just want to pull you
closer to me.

To feel your warmth against my skin.
Sometimes I want more.

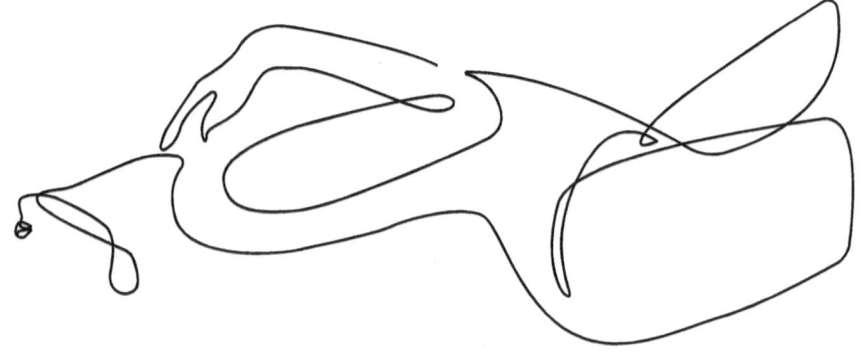

Deter, v.

You don't have to say *no*
with your words.
You say enough
with everything else.

Clasping my body while
pushing me away with your eyes.
Love became a fever
with no end in sight.

Vacant, adj.

I stare at these empty walls
where you used to hang photos
of us with friends laughing
and smiling at inside jokes.

It feels like the walls don't deserve
to be filled with light and love
if you deemed that I don't either.

Overflowing, adj.

The words fall off the page
bleeding through my intention.
Will this ever truly define
everything you meant to me?
The best I can do is try.
Will it be enough for you?

Vacillate, v.

The only thing I ever doubted,
the only thing I ever wavered on
was not forgiving you,
or letting you back into our home.

It was whether or not
there was anything else
I could have done to save you.

Resolute, adj.

You insisted that I not follow you
The Night you left. You pushed
me away, ignoring my pleas.

The last time I ever saw you
is shrouded in the black of night
and the sirens of my memory.

Valuable, adj.

You acted like the shattering of my only family heirloom wasn't a big deal.

Trifling, adj.

At a certain point I realized
that nothing I said mattered.
You took my silence as acceptance.

Victorious, adj.

It was the first argument
I ever won.
I wish I remembered
what it was about.

Subdued, adj.

I winked and grabbed
your crimson scarf.[20]
This time it's my turn.

Voluntary, adj.

Once I noticed that I was
always the first to lean
in for a kiss, I stopped trying.

Compulsory, adj.

I chuckled. *It's the law.*[21] *You have to!* I flipped the toilet paper roll over the correct way.

---

21 See *Upset* pg. 248

Wax, n. and v.

Do we grow together
at the rate of the celestial bodies?
Do we harmonize together
at the speed of sound?

***Wane**, v.*

How does something
so intangible as love
dwindle so incrementally
that eventually it becomes only
a phase?

Wealth, n.

We dreamed, not of gold
but of stability and happiness.

Poverty, n.

It never mattered that
none of our furniture matched,
or if we ate from dollar store plates.

All that mattered was
we were discovering life together
and finding joy, wherever it was.

Wild, adj.

It was the eagerness in your eyes,
the smirk in your smile,
the skip in your step,
that told me life with you
was going to be an adventure.

Tame, adj.

Years passed.
We worked well together for so long,
like a well-oiled machine
of bills, chores, and healthy meals.
When did we forget to live?

Wise, adj.

Does wisdom come
from anywhere besides
a mountain of
painful experience?

Foolish, adj.

Is it wrong
to keep forgiving you,
or am I showing a strength
you do not possess?

Worthy, adj.

I'm not even sure how to define
this monumental word anymore.
Is it the value others place upon you?
Or is how you see yourself
what truly matters?

Fraudulent, adj.

Nothing destroys a man as
quickly as making him believe
he isn't deserving of you.
He will spend the rest
of his life unlearning this lie.

Xanthippe, n.

How did I get this far without mentioning your mother?

Grace, n.

Is it egotistical
to remind you
of my mother?

Xeric, adj.

I'm not sure which was worse.
My chicken, or the way
you joked about it.

Moist, adj.

It's so strange that
so many people can have
such a visceral reaction
to a word.

But it's perfect
for kissing, the base
expression of love.

Xenial, adj.

This time we invited coworkers
to Thanksgiving. Wine flowed
like a conversation: rich and smooth.
We were the perfect hosts.

The arguing began as soon as they left.

Surly, *adj.*

I saw the signs,
knew the signals that meant
you needed time to unwind.

I hate the holiday season.

Xenophobic, adj.

It didn't take long
for me to dislike your father
as much you do.

Impartial, adj.

When you first asked me
what color to paint
the bedroom, I honestly
had no opinion.
I do now.

Xiphoid, adj.

How
crazy is
it that we
revert to Greek
or Latin just to describe
something as accurately as
possible? Like the curved
edge of your chest as
you sleep. It's not
a scimitar, it's
something
else
entirely.

Gaunt, adj.

It was the last time I saw
my grandfather.
We sat in the tiny trailer
and waited for him to
remember who I was.

Y

Yearning, n.

At the end of the day,
I just can't stand being alone.

***Negligent**, adj.*

You forgot to pick me up from work.
I stood in the rain for hours.

Yin,[24] **n.**

I want
to drink from your pool
and blend
until our souls touch

Let me find
heaven
inside your eyes

---
24 Blend together as one poem.

―――― **_Yang, n._**

―――― to swim in your veins,
―――― consume all of you,
―――― us together,
―――― hearts beating as one.

―――― the colors of
―――― hell
―――― inside us.

Yoke, n.

Tether me at the neck.
Work me to the bone.
Pray I don't escape.

***Unhinged*, adj. and v.**

Tell me the truth
just this once.
Is it duality that we fear?

Cracking your jaw or
mind wide open.
It scares me how unstable
a "silver tongue" can be.

You, pro.

How do I even begin
to put you into words?
I guess this will have to do.

Me, pro.

How do I even begin
without sounding conceited?
The devil is in the details.

Youth, n.

"Rejoice in the wife of your youth."
I had that Bible verse[22] underlined
and would read it every morning,
wondering how to make it come true.

---

[22] Proverbs 5:18 ESV

Senile, adj.

I'm sorry he[23] started forgetting before you ever got your apology.

---

23 See *Keen* pg. 122

Zany, adj.

We sat on the couch giggling.
Seriously, what's a random hill you'll die on?
You got very serious and whispered,
Snickerdoodles taste like disappointment.

Sensible, adj.

Your eyes gleamed as bright as
the shiny new paint job.
See, it's not only safe but pretty too!
Our new car, ready for a growing family.

Zap, v.

I call it the "almost kiss".
Hovering near each other,
lips half an inch apart.
The first one to move loses.
Or is that a win?

Linger, v.

The electricity stays in the air
long after we part ways.
Is this love or just chemistry?

Zealous, adj.

I recited your creed
of what it meant to love.
Etched it on my skin.[25]
Seared it on my mind.

---

25 Song of Solomon 8:6

Aloof, adj.

I should have noticed sooner
how cold you'd become.
Holding you in my arms
you wouldn't look up at me.
Please don't turn away.
Please look up.

Zeitgeist, n.

How do you distill down
an entire lifetime,
entire relationship,
entire marriage into one word?
Trust.

Contemporary, adj.

We couldn't afford the
newest fashion,
not on our small salary.
But you made it work
with thrift stores.
You turned vintage into vogue.

Zenith, n.

I saw the twinkle in your eye
as I kneeled down,[26]
and offered you the ring.
You whispered, *Yes!*

My heart skipped a beat
and I knew I
would love you for
the rest of our lives.

---

26 See *Romantic* pg. 210

Nadir, n.

As I fall to my knees,
I hear the crunch of metal from
That Night, the car accident[27]
that claimed both your lives.

I will never know if the baby was mine or *his*.
I will never hear its cry or see its face.
I never thought it would be
the last time I ever saw you.

---

27 See *Abandon* pg. 2

The End

Appendix

1. Hughes, Langston. "Let America Be America Again." *Poets.org*, https://poets.org/poem/let-america-be-america-again.

2. Whitman, Walt. "The Walt Whitman Archive." *FAST ANCHOR'D ETERNAL O LOVE! (Leaves of Grass (1881–1882)) - The Walt Whitman Archive*, https://whitmanarchive.org/published/LG/1881/poems/80.

3. Plath, Sylvia. "Mad Girl's Love Song by Sylvia Plath." *By Sylvia Plath - Famous Poems, Famous Poets. - All Poetry*, https://allpoetry.com/Mad-Girl's-Love-Song.

4. *God forbid! If that were so, how could God judge the world?* Romans 3:6 (KJV)

7. *Love is a smoke made with the fume of sighs,/ Being purg'd, a fire sparkling in lovers' eyes,*

   Romeo and Juliet Act 1 Scene 1 Lines 167-9

8. "Meanwhile, the older son was in the field. When he came near the house, he heard music and dancing. So he called one of the servants and asked him what was going on. 'Your brother has come,' he replied, 'and your father has killed the fattened calf because he has him back safe and sound.'

"The older brother became angry and refused to go in. So his father went out and pleaded with him. But he answered his father, 'Look! All these years I've been slaving for you and never disobeyed your orders. Yet you never gave me even a young goat so I could celebrate with my friends. But when this son of yours who has squandered your property with prostitutes comes home, you kill the fattened calf for him!'

"'My son,' the father said, 'you are always with me, and everything I have is yours. But we had to celebrate and be glad, because this brother of yours was dead and is alive again; he was lost and is found.'" Luke 15:25-32 (NIV)

12. *Be this the whetstone of your sword, let grief/*

   Convert to anger; blunt not the heart, enrage it.

   Macbeth Act 4 Scene 3 Lines 228-9

14. *I understand a fury in your words,/*

But not the words.

Othello Act 4 Scene 2 Lines 32-3

25. *Place me like a seal over your heart, like a seal on your arm; for love is as strong as death, its jealousy unyielding as the grave. It burns like blazing fire, like a mighty flame.* Song of Solomon 8:6 (NIV)

www.ingramcontent.com/pod-product-compliance
Lightning Source LLC
Chambersburg PA
CBHW031057080526
44587CB00011B/718